DOCUMENTS

Winner, 2018 A. Poulin, Jr. Poetry Prize
Selected by D. A. POWELL

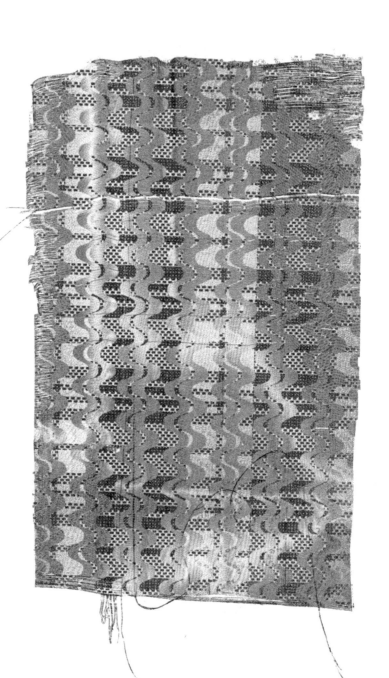

DOCUMENTS
JAN-HENRY GRAY

FOREWORD BY D. A. POWELL

A. POULIN, JR. NEW POETS OF AMERICA SERIES, NO. 42

BOA EDITIONS, LTD. — ROCHESTER, NY — 2019

First Edition
19 20 21 22 7 6 5 4 3 2 1

For information about permission to reuse any material from this book, please contact The Permissions Company at www.permissionscompany.com or e-mail permdude@gmail.com.

Publications by BOA Editions, Ltd.—a not-for-profit corporation under section 501 (c) (3) of the United States Internal Revenue Code—are made possible with funds from a variety of sources, including public funds from the Literature Program of the National Endowment for the Arts; the New York State Council on the Arts, a state agency; and the County of Monroe, NY. Private funding sources include the Max and Marian Farash Charitable Foundation; the Mary S. Mulligan Charitable Trust; the Rochester Area Community Foundation; the Ames-Amzalak Memorial Trust in memory of Henry Ames, Semon Amzalak, and Dan Amzalak; and contributions from many individuals nationwide. See Colophon on page 96 for special individual acknowledgments.

Cover Design: Sandy Knight
Cover Art: "Magic Eye" by Jonathan Molina-Garcia
Interior Design and Composition: Richard Foerster
BOA Logo: Mirko

Library of Congress Cataloging-in-Publication Data

Names: Gray, Jan-Henry, author.
Title: Documents / Jan-Henry Gray ; Forward By D. A. Powell.
Description: First edition. | Rochester, NY : BOA Editions, Ltd., [2019] | Series: A. Poulin, Jr. New Poets of America Series ; No. 42 | Includes bibliographical references.
Identifiers: LCCN 2018050082 (print) | LCCN 2018051623 (ebook) | ISBN 9781942683759 (ebook) | ISBN 9781942683742
Classification: LCC PS3607.R3945 (ebook) | LCC PS3607.R3945 A6 2019 (print) | DDC 811/.6—dc23
LC record available at https://lccn.loc.gov/2018050082

BOA Editions, Ltd.
250 North Goodman Street, Suite 306
Rochester, NY 14607
www.boaeditions.org
A. Poulin, Jr., Founder (1938–1996)

CONTENTS

FOREWORD: Documents Unsealed

to make an art from documents
that twin a life to mine.
　　　　　　　—Jan-Henry Gray

Open me a refuge where I may be renewed.
　　　　　　　—Muriel Rukeyser

When he was still a minor, Jan-Henry Gray learned from his parents that he lacked legal status in the country he had known as home since he was six. Born in Quezon City, Philippines, Gray had immigrated with his parents to the United States. And though they worked hard to provide for their family, they had been underequipped to jump through and over all the legal hoops and hurdles of immigration. For years, Jan-Henry dealt with attorneys and officials to get his official work authorization and an eventual green card, working in restaurants and putting himself through school. Though he was ineligible for federal financial aid, Gray did manage—thanks to the DREAM Act—to apply for and receive awards and scholarships for his studies, completing an AA degree at City College of San Francisco, a BA at San Francisco State University, and an MFA at Columbia College Chicago. In addition to cooking in award-winning restaurants, Jan-Henry worked at Project Open Hand, a nonprofit organization feeding homebound people such as the elderly and those living with HIV/AIDS. He also studied cinema and experimented with documentary and dramatic forms in his own short films.

Rarely would I chose to begin a discussion of someone's poetry by delving into their biography. But as concerns this particular collection, these biographical facts are the supporting architectural elements upon which the house is built. The collection is both a documentary and a documentation organized around facts and necessities, forgeries and truths. Court cases and legislative battles—and their ensuing ripples across the social fabric—pull at the substance of this book's art. What is the difference between disclosure and admission? Between hiding and omitting? These distinctions matter fundamentally in relation to *identity*, a commodity that can be stolen, erased or threatened with sanctions both legal and social.

In the long, troubled history of democratic governments and institutions, the rights and privileges of citizenship have been withheld many times and from many groups. If this is a free country, why does it cost so much? And why is it that some people pay more than others—with their labor and with their lives—and still get the short pile. It is not the duty of poetry to affirm inequality; indeed, art, if it is to be of any use, must constantly challenge the assumptions of the society in which it is made.

For, unlike other products, art does not need capitalism in order to be valued. Its merit is its ability to get at truths that monetary systems ignore and obfuscate in order to maintain dynamics of power. The structure of such systems, when they favor disproportionate distribution of wealth, must be undermined by those most affected. Writes Gray, "early, / I learn how to lie on forms."

Forms are broken, modified, reimagined, and interrogated, as if they themselves are under investigation for possible illegalities. "Bring an interpreter," an official "Notice of Action" demands. "What's his father's name" and "what's *his* father's name."

One of the deep ironies of economic disparity is that those who are least advantaged often must take menial jobs caring for those who are most advantaged. It is a kind of sickness that keeps one side of the social scale from destroying the other, bound together as they are by mutual need. And so the poor and disenfranchised become the caretakers, nannies, nurses, waiters, delivery drivers, parking attendants. In a series of poems spread throughout the book, Gray speaks about the lives of maids. "Each note describes 'One Thing Done Well' during that pay cycle. The envelope may also include an image of you documenting that moment; images culled from the surveillance footage." In other poems, immigrants are literally inscribed by their own diasporas ("I met a Caribbean girl named after an African country at the bakery") or given separate entrances to separate lives:

THE FAMILY moves into THE GARAGE.
THE FAMILY lives there for THE YEAR.
THE GARAGE is underneath THE HOUSE.

Running contiguously to the narrative of seeking legal status as an immigrant is the quest for legal status within a same-sex relationship in the years leading up to and immediately following the court decisions on marriage equality. "Two boys, rings on their fingers, buying flowers in a strange town." Applying for recognition as his husband's spouse, the narrator is asked "how much does he make" and informed "we may videotape you." The queer body, the brown body, the immigrant body . . . is this body not granted the same right to privacy guaranteed by the equal protection clause of the Fourteenth Amendment and the First Amendment to the US Constitution? This is a battle still being fought in the courts of a country promising freedom and equality under the law. Whose law is it. Who gets refuge on these shores.

Documents opens every closet and drawer and says search me. It says "[hide History]" It is a full disclosure and a redaction, a history and its endless revisions.

—D. A. Powell

horizon—a permanent humiliation on the act of arrival

egress

you are the red dot
on the glass over the map
your fingers trace a path
from entrance to exit

you are the sound inside
a sleeping body
a family of six
a car stalled
the hazards blinking

we never don't look over our shoulders
every form, a trick question
every map, a trap street
we huddle to inspect the smoke
rising from the engine

Maid Poem #1: The Housemaid

In the center of the concrete room there is a pink plastic water basin, wobbly, full, and brimming. On its side is a faded sticker of a smiling elephant with a fat ribbon around its neck. Three boys, wearing only shorts, sweating, stand around half-daring each other to jump over the basin without breaking its water. Outside, the housemaid, faded floral duster, a scar underneath her eye, lines empty soda bottles with the tops cut off side by side along the wall to the back door. In them go soil or rocks or rainfall. She sits on a miniature chair. She is waiting for stormcloud, homecoming, miracle, or for one of the naked boys to run toward her, their open mouths full of blood and laughing. And when the bark of the dog rises from the other side, her eyes dart to the fence—to a gap from plank to plank just large enough for a dog's head but not hers. She knows this. On the day she tried, the dog, a smudge of black and brown, flanked by wild grass, no leash, hungry, rose to its three legs and did not bark.

April 1984

The young mother   born
    with the wrong name
        boards a plane.
Flanked by
    her second   and   third child,
she squeezes the last
    of the honey from the plastic packet
and stirs
    her tea
      not   with the flimsy stick
           handed to her   by the pink stewardess
but with her own stubborn finger
    ignorant   of etiquette   or the gossip
      gathering in the rows behind her.

The young mother   does not check
    her watch
    during any   of the   19 hours
        her first flight   her first time
      over the Pacific Ocean—
      that blue expanse on the map from
          Manila to Milkenhoney, California.

She watches white
    cartoon clouds
      out of the oval window
  practices her English
    wiggles in the heat of
    her cloth corset   to hide her size
and keeps   a flat hand
  on her belly
  as if to say
    soon   enough   soon enough.

          In three weeks, her last child,
     small-eyed   his skin   lighter than the others

will be born:
> he will hear   the clatter   of two languages
>   stories   about home   from the others and
>   cry for his mother's milk.

XXX-XX-0142

momma takes aim. leans into the machine. types
my first social security card. her third try. early,
I learn how to lie on forms.

REQUEST FOR APPLICANT TO APPEAR FOR INITIAL INTERVIEW

APPLICATION NUMBER MSC XXXXXXX058

A# A XXX XXX 961

Notice Date: July 24, 2014

Priority Date: July 24, 2014

Date of Arrival: February 20, 1984

hereby notified to appear
  how often do you have sex
to adjust status
  what color is his toothbrush
his birth certificate
  what side of the bed does he sleep on
resident alien
  how much does he make
your husband must come with you
  what's his mother's name
we may videotape you
  where did you buy your rings
bring an interpreter
  what are his siblings' spouses' names
in a sealed envelope bring
  what's his father's name
failure to appear
  what's *his* father's name
please appear, as scheduled below

  do you love him
supporting evidence
  why do you love him
Tuesday, March 17, 2015 8:00am USCIS Chicago, IL

don't mention citizenship
talk about love, how you got married for love

Missing Document

February 1984/ Quezon City/ Philippines
Documents: copies of I-94 (missing)
Supporting Information: flight number/ date of departure/ seat numbers of the family
    members (missing)

"tell the story of somewhere else"
ISBN 978-1-56689-173-8

"I had a taste for ambiguity
& arrival"
ISBN 978-1-56478-184-0

her hand did not wave / her hand was ice / ice set to the temperature of the air / the air between the sand pressed to make the glass / the glass window she stood behind / next to the door / the wood door / the heavy wood door that I can't say for sure was oak / but am certain was

heavy / oiled / ridged / with a gold doorknob that looked like what we were told gold looked like / gold the color not the ore / not Au or $ or what fills the vaults in the movies my mother's father watches on a sunday / awake in the 6am 5am 4am dark / his cigarette burning / a kind of dying / orange / sunrise / light /

her hand / her hand against the glass / my mother's sisters' hands / or maybe they were maya deren's hands / something's getting in the way / can't say / for certain / my mother's name is rebecca // focus // tell us about her hand // what do you see // ground us // in the work // the details / go there / really take us somewhere

Balikbayan

A balikbayan box or "repatriate box" is a package of items. Sometimes shipped by sea, these boxes are often sent by air with a Filipino returning to the Philippines.

[hide History] [edit these boxes] Fill with what the sender thinks the recipient would like: non-perishable food, toiletries, household items, electronics, toys, items (American) hard to find Medium: 18 x 16 x 18 Large: 18 x 18 x 24 Extra large: 24 x 18 x 24 inches 75 pounds max. Benefit of bulk versus individual. Tradeoff: long transit time, lack of delivery date. Returnees are expected to bring home gifts to family and friends—the practice of pasalubong.[1] Work overseas as maids in Saudi, in a brothel in Dubai, or nurses in the States [citation needed] Ever since Typhoon Ketsana (now ~~Haiyan~~ no Yolanda) and Homeland Security: almost all shipments have been delayed.

1

Across the Pacific Ocean

*

To stand still
is to sink in sand.

*

Swim past the buoy where the guard can't see.

*

In the photograph that you show me every holiday
we have the same conversation about
eating guavas on the beach, the black sand, and
when when when I will go back.

*

Painted blue and slate and
white from corner to corner,
the ocean extends past
the canvas edge. I hang
it backwards to see
the art behind the art.

*

At the ruins of the Sutro Baths.
100 years ago, people met
there and nowhere else.

*

It was here
where we learned how
to be naked around other bodies.

*

At dawn, gulls command and will the day.
Then, the machinery of the city—
its beaming commerce burns off all fog.
The ocean brings it back. She cannot sleep.

*

August 16, 2013:
One kilometer from your
port of call, two ships collide
in the middle of the night.
The hull of the ferry Thomas Aquinas
is now a mouthless whale.
Children slept in her belly.
And there were others . . .

*

How do you weigh an ocean?

*

I have no poems for the Atlantic.
Or New York. Or Europe either.
I look westward:
from home to home.

*

On the plane, I ate cubed fruit from a plastic cup.
I drank true milk. I looked out the window,
learned to pronounce my names
and how to spell them.

*

The only way to know a song is to sing it.
The only way to know the ocean is to swim it.

*

I cannot wait any longer for the tides to rise to me.

Mackerel

Today was mackerel, nets full of them.
Silver as christmas tinsel, their fins a foil origami in the sea.

Down in the market, bronzed women sell bits of shell,
Prices hand-scrawled on cardboard with charcoal with chalk.

In the bars where only Spanish is spoken,
There is talk of the new cannery.

The subject of the season thrills the oldest women.
Remembering when they were little, they gather and giggle.

Some are missing teeth, others have silver crowns.
They have shouldered strong children.

The women sit, eat, and wipe bread crumbs from the table with
the backs of their broad forearms onto their laps and onto the floor
for no one to clean up.

A woman walks in with a wooden box of shelling beans.
They are large pods, gray-green, flatter than favas.

Behind the women, in an empty kitchen, a pot of salted water boils.
salt the water   see how it tastes   like the ocean

Between my hands, I toy with a cup empty for half an afternoon.
The plate of beans is brought to the table:

Steaming, whole, without labor.
Tonight is mackerel. Cold potatoes. Squat glasses of purple wine.

See how they eat the beans.
See how they peel the pods back.

Maid Poem #2

We were shown how to eat with our hands, how to pick the meat between bones, how to feel for the small slivers hidden in fish, how to gather food with four fingers and push it into our mouths with our thumbs.

There were no knives at our table, those were kept in the back kitchen, with the maids. They ate when we ate. They stayed back when we went to church, to tend to the chickens, to care for the youngest, always sick.

We knew their names, the smell of their skin. Shame I can't name them now. My mother remembers them all and each, which maid was paired with which child and which one (only one) would come with us when we went to the mountain to ride horses in the fog.

A Migration

after James Wright's "A Blessing"

On the way to Baguio City
Mountain fog surrounds our parked car.
10,000 horses and their nostrils
Press upon a single gate
Breathing their animal sickness.
They've smelled the new grass as
We wipe the windows and look to the horizon
Where they too have set their eyes.
They nudge the gate, collect their weight on the fence.
With or without witness,
They huddle like cattle. Their love is theirs alone.
There is no ambivalence in animal attention.
On the other side, the oldest begin
To die. The yearlings guard the bones.
I would like to hold in my hand this image:
The closed gate opening,
My left hand lifting the latch—
Black, brown, gray, white, spotted,
Freed legs in the new wildness.
The charged air of their galloping,
Their skins rippled on ribs like a lake
First finding its shore.

There are no conclusions
Better than the ones that came before.

In "The Store with Beautiful Things"

I wander the aisles
        listless
            in shoplift,
        knee-deep
            in trinkets.

I shop for things not worth keeping
            with cut-out coupons for
                plastic wrapped in plastic,
                    cassette tape carousels,
            and honorable mentions.

The clerk with a name too beautiful for this world
            sees me in line,
                four deep
            a sadsack
        holding a bag of melting ice
                    and waves me over.

            In a Spanish only we understand
                I say I'm stranded
                    with a jittery compass
                        pointing me to nowhere in particular.

I make announcements so loud they become true:
                The Philippines is ghost-country!
                And the island we left
                has been sinking
            one inch
            every
            year
            for the
        last
        one
    thousand
years.

I tell him that
  the door labeled WC
    stands for *who cares?* and that
      civilization stopped using closets weeks ago.

It happened
    on a midweek afternoon
        without pomp or circumstance,
            without preamble or prediction.
There is no archive
        no livestream
              for the day everything changed.

Now, in our new iteration,
I need certain certainties like the choir kneels to listen.
        I lift my palms upwards, as if to say:

Let us sing a song made up of a single word.

              And the Word,
      it   can   be   anything:

                    like jigsaw
                    like peanut
                    like heartbeat
                    like Amen
                    like bingo
                    like crisscross
                    like dripdrop
                    like shipshape
                    like rowboat
                    or rickshaw
                    or crisscross
                    or singsong
                    or frogleg
                    or ticktock
                    or halo
                    or seashore
                    or comeback
                    or gohome

Maid Poem #3: Before a Feast for Maids

What do you want
to eat? I don't know
what you like. The others.
What do they want?
How many
are you? Can your
husband come?
Your sister? Or
sisters. How many?
How old is she? Your
mother. Can you bring
her? The others
will bring their families
too. How many
are you? Can you
bring another table
out? I want you all
to eat together.
In the big room,
not in the kitchen,
not a regular party.
Do you think
they will be comfortable
here? Should I send the car?
How many are you?
Is there anything
you can't have? How old
are you? You're
a woman now. Your father?
Is he still sick? That's good.
Have you seen the dentist?
Should I send you? So you can
enjoy too. Your daughter.
Again, what's her name?
What does she
like? Not you. The others

can set up the tables
out there. Out
in the garden. If
it doesn't rain. If I tie up
the dogs. The whole family.
All of them. How many
are you? Of course.
Don't worry about that. Wear
what you want. We're all the same.
Bring them all. I can
make arrangements.
I don't want you
to clean up.
On a Sunday.
After church.
I will send the car.
Where is your church?
Not too far.
Good. Good.
This is for you.
All of you.
No work.
Just a party.
The families
having a nice time.
And food.
And so many desserts.
American desserts.
Anything you want.
This is for you.
All of us.

Maid Poem #4: The Day of the Feast for Maids

It rained. The car was late. We wore our best. We waited in the entryway of the church. The next mass was beginning. The usher told us there were plenty of seats. *Come inside*, he said with his hands. *We are okay here*, I said with mine.

My mother is tired. I gave her a small piece of paper with the names of the other maids. Above the names, I underlined one name. I told her she was nice to us.

The church doors opened. *I got lost on my way,* the driver said. We huddled under umbrellas, water falling on our shoulders. Inside the car, we could see nothing through the dark windows. My mother slept and I closed my eyes. The sound of rain.

In the front driveway of the house, I could smell food I did not cook. *Come inside,* she said, *come inside.* We put our wet shoes with the other wet shoes. She grabbed me by the arm and showed me to the table. She pointed at every dish: *Look! Lechon. Sugpo. Oxtail kare-kare. Bicol express. Morcon with two kinds of sausage, Chinese and Portuguese. Garlic crab. Nice bread. Baguette. Spaghetti for the kids. Barbecue. Shiapao, two kinds. The kids, where are they? Beef empanadas. And paella Filipina with squid, mussels, and blood sausage. Look at the desserts, come here.*

As a girl, I was taught how to care for others. Here, what can my mother eat? The roads back will be full of mud and the bottom of the car will get dirty. I should have asked for soup, something for her to eat.

In the Fields, I Learned a Hymn

I.

He teaches me to *mix cement quick in the shade.*
He presses my ears to the concrete.
I hear a testament tune & *close your eyes for good.*
Churchgirl sells cassava cake *but don't buy.*
She unhooks her hair from her mouth & knows.
Shake it off, his smell, the flies, the sky turning purple,
an opened jar of palm sugar, *the house is sleeping.*
The path is marked by years of feet. See him
shortcut through the grass. I come for what is mine.
He bends my body: *Boy, cool my knuckles in the new soil—*
where it's soft. Soft & black with life.

II.

> *quick in the shade*
> *close your eyes*
> *but don't*
> *take it off*
> *take what is mine*
> *through the grass*
> *these hours are for sleeping*
> *cool my knuckles boy*
> *bury me in the new soil*

III.

Teach me. Press me into the testament tune, cassava, palm sugar, cake, opened jar.
See him, his smell, the flies, the sky turning purple. The churchgirl's hair in his
mouth. The path is marked by years of feet. Bend my body where its soft and black.

Sapling

A young tree bears avocados, their pits heavy as boulders. Nearby, tufts of grass worm with life. A boy tucks a dull knife into the small of his hand to shave off the tree's first, then second, layer. Mindless, he does this from morning to noon—until the gardener boy arrives aglow, his hair a sun-baked crown of toil. He enters the garden with tools, a bag of broken bones. The sun is in zenith; there are no shadows. Only what is done. One boy gestures the other to the metal shed. In that tin box of dust and little breathing, their bodies go. But before the door is latched, a breeze, warm as a father's hand, blows around the house, over the garden, and rushes into their sweetened, smiling mouths.

A miracle how fruits know to ripen in the summer air. Or how the wind knows to carry certain seeds from tree to tree.

d. 1997

I'm looking for you in these impossible rooms
       squinting for a flash of flesh, a mouth is a mouth—
       I grope for skin, disease, bone, pubes of loose rope.

I'm looking for you on skinny streets shaded by
       Chinatown brick, all alleys lead to dead ends,
       find a door, lose the ghost, take the narrow stairs
       to silver, seaweed, bleach, and Japanese steam.

I'm looking for you in the heated eucalyptus, tile, and pine.
       Is that you, the old man slumped in the sauna
       making small talk and spying?

I'm looking for you in this landlocked school,
       a half-brown boy between the rows
       of women with potpourri dresses and polite tattoos—
       they are earnest, learned, they say
       they love you too. (How do I tell them our story?)

I'm looking for you in the sole of my boot, the new grass, the bent tree.
       Older branches bend toward other branches, curl backward to trunk
       or downward to stump. Tender branches split so easily in two or three.
       I pause, listen, count, and look . . .

I'm looking at your small eyes when you say *let's get lost* by
       the last windmill, you pull out the bent book
       from my back pocket, toss it on the ground, and grin.
       You whisper *have you been to Lands End?* Lands End,
       two words I hear for the first time and for one eternal minute
       we disappear from this noisy century. We come back weightless,
       the sun is slow, more orange than ever.

I'm looking for you in 1997. I am 19. You are in your last year here.
       In eight months you will turn to ash, to prayer, to canon. I ditch school
       the day you're signing books at City Lights in the middle of the afternoon.
       (I tuck my copy of *Howl* in my jacket pocket and feel, in a word, absurd.)

I'm looking at your brown face, an old man behind
     a small table, and smile. Your hands are sweating
     and so are mine. You take my writing hand in yours
     and squeeze. With your other hand, you grab my
     forearm. Pink and brown, trembling, tender, and hairless still.
     We press together and don't say much. You press harder, you feel
     the pores on my arm open and open and open.

River Capture

for three voices

repeat each once, the second time
only repeat the dashed lines

1.	2.	3.
-to bend		
to mouth		
-to rock		
to run		
-to rill		
to fall		
-to flow		
to river --------------------	-to bend	
-a stream	to mouth	
-to cross	-to rock	
-to rock	to run	
to knot	-to rill	
-& meander	to fall	
-to braid	-to flow --------------------	-to bend
-to bridge	to river	-to mouth
to fall	-a stream	to rock
to field	to cross	-to run
-to flood	-to rock	-to rill
	-to knot	-to fall
-there's a river	-& meander	-to flow
-past the trees	-to braid	to river
-over the fence	to bridge	-a stream
-on the other side	-to fall	-to cross
-of the field	-to field	-to rock
	-to flood	-to knot
		& meander
	-there's a river	-to braid
	-past the trees	-to bridge
	-across the bridge	to fall
	-on the other side	to field
	-of the bend	-to flood
		-there's a river
		-filled with rocks
		-under a fallen tree
		-there's a river
		-filled with rocks
		-under a fallen tree

On Translation

A tree's branch
breaks.

A falling branch is
a branch, not a twig

until it has fallen
and is *with-the-ground*.

There, the twig
is among other twigs.

Also there, it is near
the root of its tree.

Maid Poem #5: Rita

Rita held a knife
Pa walked in the room
Ma was asleep
Pa spoke to Rita
Rita stole the money
Ma turned her head
Pa saw Rita do it
Pa locked the door
Ma ate alone
Rita hid her money
There's blood on Rita's skirt
Ma drove her home
Said *Rita pray to god*
Kissed Rita on the head
Ma cleaned the kitchen
Pa took off his shirt
Ma laid in the bed
Pa heard a noise
Ma cut the wires
Pa opened the door
There's blood on Rita's skirt
Ma held her hand
They were quiet in the room
Pa laid down to rest
Ma spoke to Rita
Whispered in her ear
Pa saw you take it
Pa took off his belt
Ma held her down
Rita prayed to god
Pa said no to Rita
Rita cooked the food
Ma said *say nothing*
Ma's fingers on the beads
Rita washed the floor
Rita on her knees

Ma lifted Rita's skirt
Pa saw Rita do it
Ma took off her belt
Pa asked for food
Rita looked at Ma
Rita watched him eat

Maid Poem #6: Proscenium

The maid crosses the courtyard and places a box of flattened cardboard boxes outside the gate. Above her head, two children, brother and little sister, press themselves on the window and wave dumbly at the birds then the squirrels scurrying up the end-of-March trees toward their dreys made of twig, spit, and popsicle sticks. The two children jump in, out, and through; tangling and untangling themselves from the curtain. It's hide-and-seek, peekaboo, tag, house, and fort. The maid is deaf to their play. She holds a red carpet at arm's length and whacks it with a broom. The dust catches the sunlight and falls to her feet. The girl is playing dead, a pacifier in her mouth. The boy stands above her with his toy gun. He puts his cold foot on her belly. The girl wiggles free and curls into the corner of the sill. She's done. He sticks his tongue out, smears a circle with it on the window, looks across the courtyard, and sees me.

California Triptych

I

To speak of
tongues like
teenage girls speak
of second base
is to know how
ever since
the big reveal
neither father
nor mother
could look at
one another
in the eye and
say in speech
as plain as day:
in the future
our journals will
fail us
our daughter will
rename herself
something chic
like *Magazine*
and our neighbors
will post a
FREE sign on
a yellowed mattress
while allergic children
sleep atop
cat blankets
warm with the
inherited wisdom that
all dogs bark
independent
of size
kingdom
or rank.

II

In the golden glow of
the postprandial hour
talk turns to temperature
and the trend in
this year's crop of
festival films with
slow meandering shots
lasting longer than
most audiences feel
comfortable watching
until their minds
turn to thoughts of
the green light bulb
that glows behind
exit signs or
their top three
favorite fonts or how
poetically unpoetic
the memoir by
a failed architect
titled *My Life as
a Failed Architect*
lays on a well-stacked
fold-out table under
an awning on a day
built for buying books
read from cover to cover
to consider to whom
it may concern
to loom to limn
to post is to lintel
as a room is a room
if all four walls
agree to meet at all
the right angles.

III

Bend your neck and
lend your good ear
to the one about
the absent father
the tardy mother and
the laughing children
who were
for one summer
left in a plastic
wading pool
without water
under the smog and
shade of the
San Gabriel Mountains
and slept with
one eye open
toward another world
toward anything else
that might come
rushing back
to find
their tiny bodies like
statues in genuflect
in the half-deflated
blow-up pool
sagging inch by inch
into the unkempt plot
which the late mother
said was a lesson that
they could only
appreciate with
time
so time
and not love
was what she gave them.

I'm a Good Person Because My Childhood Was

junk yard, Goodwill, crushed cans, buy-1-get-1-free, reruns, dead leaves in the pool, no lifeguard, landlord no English, bounced check, smog check, two—no, need three jobs, back entrance, under the table, no ride after school, loud dogs, mean neighbors, no neighbors, someone died there, FOR RENT sign, up for months, rusted carts, bruised fruit, free bones, just ask, beef tongue, chicken broth, chicken hearts, clouded eye of fish on ice, fry it extra crispy, the house smells like patis and Windex and roses from the rosewater bath to heal the kidney, traffic, church is packed, late for church, not going to church, news of a shooting, news of a robbery, news of the boy raped at prom, pictures of the teens in court, *animals!,* those crying parents, *his* crying parents, Rodney King, Reginald Denny, everyone's yelling on Ricki or Jerry or Maury or Montel and Oprah is on the cover of her own magazine, dentist office, insurance voucher, no social, permanent address, temporary address, magazines with the address torn off, *it's your first time,* the handsome dentist says, he touches you and you feel special and rich and white and American and healthy and taken care of, T.C.C.I.C., keep in touch, have a nice summer, we'll be friendz 4 forever, never change

Fine

ice in the bag, bag in the drawer, spare key, spare change, tires on the blade, parked car, a knock on the door, steam, smoke, same, the size of a coffin, the spilled drink, the saucer and its center, shallow, the washed-up waitress, hands in her apron, fingers fingering foil, salt, lint, last week's meal in the fridge, weeping, condom in the trash, jacket on the wall, a mattress is a bed, baby's in the back, it's cold, it's winter, it's fine, the fees, the tickets, buy bulk, bloated, wallets swollen with paper, remember the letter in the lot, blades rise, tires reverse, alarm, gate closed, toll, bridge, earthquake, aftershock, school's out means make lunch, wash face, hide tools, hide bag, check door, lock door, check door, open the windows to let the smell out

The Dream Act

There is A GARAGE underneath THE HOUSE.

THE HOUSE has an address.

THE GARAGE does not.

There is A DOOR cut into the garage door.

This is the entrance for THE FAMILY.

THE GARAGE is underneath THE HOUSE.

One night, THE FATHER meets another father who owns THE HOUSE.

They talk about the place downstairs, THE GARAGE underneath THE HOUSE.

THE FAMILY moves into THE GARAGE.

THE FAMILY lives there for THE YEAR.

THE GARAGE is underneath THE HOUSE.

THE FATHER brings home A TREE.

THE FAMILY calls it A CHRISTMAS TREE.

THE TREE is propped on a table in THE GARAGE.

There is no address but there is a telephone line in THE GARAGE.

THE MOTHER is on the phone with her mother.

THE MOTHER is describing THE HOUSE.

THE GARAGE is underneath THE HOUSE.

THE CHILDREN decorate THE TREE with ornaments made of paper.

Maid Poem #7: HR

At the Maid Museum, we honor the many who have cooked meals in other people's kitchens, washed floors, labored on holidays, nursed the frail, and tended the children. The Maid Museum houses art commemorating Maid Culture by the best artists of our time. On exhibit are wall-sized paintings, large-scale photography—even sculpture and installation. Artifacts, letters, and other ephemera are preserved and on display in the temperature-controlled galleries. Our docents are robust, learned, but unrobotic. They have mastered the pronunciations of all of the Maids' names. Doing so is required research and research is synonymous with interest which we value here. The Museum is free. We are open 24 hours to accommodate the many faiths and habits in our community. The coffee is good and strong and you will agree. Tea is served on every floor. Lunch too is good. There are complimentary house-made pickles and free refills. All of our employees have health insurance so that getting sick is not also shameful. Uniforms are provided. There is ride-share, snow days, sick days, paid vacation, direct deposit, and a generous R&D budget. On payday at The Maid, every employee receives a brown envelope with a handwritten letter by one of the poets-in-residence thanking them for their service. Each note describes "One Thing Done Well" during that pay cycle. The envelope may also include an image of you documenting that moment; images culled from the surveillance footage. The Maid Museum is currently hiring. All applicants are welcome. We are an EOE.

Terminal Couplet

for airports

Twelve straight months of metal rain.
Paused, they wait in peopled stages:
A womb, a room, a train to plane
And pass the time—aging is ageless.
Virgins sip sodas with husbands while wives
Slip something *it's nothing* in whisky and water.
He melts into *The Story of Our Lives*
And Mira sends her last text to her father.
Dry-mouthed, standing shoulder to shoulder,
They watch the carousel spit out black bags
And mumble *not mine* over and over.
Josef, six, red backpack, changes his name to John on his tag.
And the plane, still, idle on the tarmac, has lost her wings.
The blind pilot, one day, will sing a song about these things.

Love Poem with a Hole in It

"I cannot take lightly the thought of other people having sex without me"
           —*Poison* dir. Todd Haynes

to feel/useful/to be/of use/a fuck of white & pink & brown & black boys
full of use/fuel/men & men/mouth on mouth/bruised to swollen
slung & huffing/bloodshot & gone/a body/crushed/a scrum/tongues on thighs
a pair of pliant logs for legs/use a fist first/shove his head down
another hole/to use/to feed/a need to be/of use/to feel used/used up
worn/warm/him on him & me/wanting/to use every useable inch of me
tear in half/a whole/go/put the thing in me
come & king me/make a useful night of me

Hindi Ko Alam Ng Sasabihin Ko

your mother shops for fish
> a plastic bag for a glove

you untangle the wires with the crew
> a boy among men

you choose the photograph for the wake
> a finger in your mouth

you tied the string too tight
> you were poor but happy

you don't know what to say
> a balloon's string strung on your wrist

you watch your mother in the blue-black kitchen
> men sag to touch the dancing boys

in the hospital full of Filipina nurses
> dry palm trees rustle in the Santa Ana winds

she grips her ankle on the floor
> you ask what to say and how to say it

she takes her wig off and lights a candle
> to clear the spirits from the room

For Tanzania

I met a Caribbean girl named after an African country at the bakery she worked at on a tree-lined street the year I lived in Seattle. One day, she decided to stop raising her eyebrows when speaking to customers. *Raising your eyebrows is what West Coast girls do when they are being fake-nice.* I asked her if she liked it better here or there. She couldn't say. Instead, she told me a story about taking a trip to New York last summer with her first white girlfriend. They were walking from the park toward Harlem. Her girlfriend wore shorts. Her pale legs shone bright in the darkening street like the worst kind of neon. They walked next to each other. They did not hold hands. She was embarrassed for her. Embarrassed for her legs. Wished it wasn't so dark out. Wished it was winter, wet, Seattle, everybody covered up from head to toe. They walked the next six long blocks, silent, as if on a vast mound on the moon.

PNW

Hear the rustling
of fallen leaves
beneath. The ear
can see what

the feet can't feel—
the bridge inside the
season's song: yellow
yellow gold, orange

orange red. A leaf
coppering, bronzing,
bronzed, browned
to gold then back to

brown to soil, the
crush of leaves. Say
Snoqualmie Falls
and all the little s's

of Issaquah. Use your
hands to pronounce
Enumclaw. Eat eggs
after midnight without

worry. Go north.
Then, even further
north. At the table sit
two Madeleines. One

who smiles, one you
name Emily. Take his
hand. Smell sardines on
his fingers, cinnamon

doughnuts on his neck.
Together, think of
the *n* at the end
of the Ocean. And

further in, the Sound.
Where you are. Here
is a boy named Alex,
the bar with the booths

he carves his name into
backwards. He stops after
the first-last letter: X
The flame is red and

orange and yellow.
Closer to the wood,
it's a different color. Is
it blue? It rained for

sixty-eight straight
days and nights.
What you have heard,
I've heard too.

Crush, Supermarket, California

It's easy to
fall in love
with the
grocery store boys—
the one with the
tiny coffee cup
sweatshirt, too-tight
pants & cotton shoes or
the impossibly pale
fish boy who smiles
when he says, *I'm
from Alaska.* Your
heart swelled,
stupid &
dreaming
of a boat
in arctic
waters,
stars,
dots
that
dot the
ocean floor, you
will read
him poems & he
will explain the code
in the constellation
until morning
waking together,
hunting for
no fish, sailing
as you two do,
parallel
only to
each other,

listening to ice
melt
back
to water.

EXAQUA

On his first day in a new country,
he walked from water to water, as if to test the boundaries.

—Jennifer S. Cheng

feels like it allows for greater
breadth/depth . . . I'm curious, what does the form free up? I'm not certain. I used
to think that poetry = freedom. Freedom out of the sentence, proper
grammar, or reasoned reasoning. I used to think that a poem, more than
other types of writing, allowed for leaps, disjunction, mystery, even
magic. I thought that the poem was the best (and cheapest) way to
create collage. There's the poem as machine. The poem as sketch. As
document. As a walk. As a conversation with oneself. As writing that
cannot be paraphrased. There was a lot that drew me toward poetry but,
being immersed in it

I've begun to grow fatigued. I've learned that writing poems is possible and possibility diminishes exploration. When I arrive elsewhere, say, to the essay, I feel at play. I feel like I have come upon new toys with no instructions. I wander. I hold at an idea longer. I think freer. I don't look for the exit door as quickly as I would in a poem. It lets me explore the wildness that I initially found so exciting in poetry. *So, in that sense, our trajectories are similar, just going in opposite directions. Exhausted, the essay brought me to poetry. And for you, exhausted, poems are bringing you to the essay.* Then, there's the artless essay, the dreaded personal statement. The last one read: I intend to contribute to the seldom-told narrative of living as an undocumented Filipino-American whose path to citizenship is tied up with another politicized modern moment: the legalization of gay marriage. As a corporeal intersection of both undocumented and queer identities, my body is seen by many as unnatural—a site of horror, a target of the phobic. As such, two major threats loom over the project: the risk of sexually transmitted diseases on the gay male body and deportation for the undocumented non-citizen. For many who share my unique position, the desire for state-sanctioned citizenship is analogous to the cure for HIV, two statuses that are, for now, locked in a utopian vision—objects on the horizon.

It often feels like I am swimming or at least orbiting and poems feel like I am pausing or resting. Water is the medium, the texture, the space, the weight, the motion/emotion of your writing/thinking. Would you agree? Is that too tidy? Your work is attuned to water and being close to it (or, better, being inside it) is important to you. *Sure, we share the desire to never be too far from it. There's a fear of being landlocked.* The rhetorical shape of the sestina, say, is a six-bursted star. The thinking is circular, essayistic. How does one describe the urgent approach to an object? If there is an unknown object (x), the movement toward that object is circular. Much like how a DOG approaches another animal it has never smelled before. The DOG circles, smells, susses, forms an idea, decides, barks, or walks away.

$x = why$ (bad joke). *There is space between the hands. There is space between the hands and space around the hands. There is space around the hands and space in the room. There is space in the room that surrounds the shapes of everyone's hands and body and feet and cells and the beating contained within. There is space, an uneven space, made by this pattern of bodies. This space goes in and out of everyone's bodies. Everyone with lungs breathes the space in and out as everyone with lungs breathes the space between the hands in and out as everyone with lungs breathes the space between the hands and the space around the hands in and out.* Juliana Spahr's poems do this. Hers is a patient poetics that *insist*. Patient persistence.

Oh, that's what I was originally thinking of with the notion of swimming or orbiting that you mentioned: a giant essay that interrupts (or cleaves?) into the book. To cleave is to separate and to bring together. To yoke. To it: I'm thinking of this essay I want to write as . . . Essay as Ocean. Not necessarily in a geographic, landscapey way but weirder, queer, dense, full of strange currents with different temperatures, something immersive, at times panicky, the feeling of losing oxygen but delighted by the sight of strange objects that litter the ocean floor. An oasis of sight. Geography textbooks and all of that richly descriptive language. How can anyone read about the unseen formation of volcanoes or the glacial creation of lakes and not feel connected to the Earth—capital E? Essay as a vast, limitless, edgeless, impossible-to-keep-in-one's-head-all-at-once phenomenon. Essay as a way of breaking up the rest of the poems that surround it. I wanted to offer a break, a reprieve. Freedom from forms.

In *Zong!*, M. NourbeSe Philip writes "Some—all the poems—need a great deal of space around them—as if there is too much cramping around them, as if they need to breathe." In the first of *Nine Stories*, a man touches the tender sole of a boy's foot. The boy runs out to the water then disappears. There are certain words to describe certain waves. Fugitive. Objects are not fugitive, the waves carrying them are. I've flown over the Pacific Ocean once—when my family moved to California when I was six. I've had my cards read, also only once, with the CHARIOT card blocking one thing from another. It was many years ago and I was maybe drunk and worse, the boy reading me the cards was someone who I was so stupidly in love with that my brain broke when we were together. I was all heart. He pointed his finger to the CHARIOT card and said something about how there must be something locked with the migration when I was six, something that still needed unlocking. He was right. He married and divorced his then-girlfriend and now he has two kids. She lives in one state, he lives in another. Some of that is still true. I arrive on the page, messy and edgeless.

Sometimes it starts with a scrap of language from the day, a draft of an email, some harmless question I foolishly answer. I'm trying to write this thing about the ocean. Or, better, I'm trying to write this thing from inside the ocean. *Do you feel like you have seen the island sinking?* Yes, I feel it sinking inch by terrible inch. On the anniversary of his mother's death, my husband brought flowers to the ocean—where she is. Today is November 4, 2015, and her grave is somewhere underneath the dry grass of South Dakota, where she was born. Once, when we visited, our rental was the only car in the lot. Past the chain-link fence was a no-name interstate. Sometimes, a car passed. There was a slight breeze. Leaves shook in the trees. I walked inside the sound of those leaves, around the cemetery, and stopped on another family's plot, their name large on every stone: BLOOM. There they were, all together: mother and father, daughter and son. And a few inches away, the sons and daughters of those sons and daughters. I thought of all the writers of obituaries, the hands that built coffins, and those who carved stones. We bought flowers that day from the only shop in town. The old Dakota couple who ran it out of their home were nice enough. I used their bathroom, washed my hands with their soap, and we thanked them on our way out. Two boys, rings on their fingers, buying flowers in a strange town. We got in the car, didn't turn the music on, let the car's hum lull us back to ourselves. We held hands and didn't stop until we got back to the air-conditioned hotel, curtains closed, and drank wine in plastic cups.

Legend has it that James Tate decided to be a poet when he crossed out the word MOUNTAIN and wrote the word VALLEY. Just like that. *I just wasn't myself. I couldn't enjoy it. I didn't know how to be.* I thought that a city like Chicago, big city as it was, would be different. I had no clue how deeply segregated it was. But, I also know you have to leave it before you can write about it. James Baldwin and his American blackness in the Swiss Alps. Have you written about your time in Iowa? *Sure. But not in any artful way. I tend to look further than that for inspiration. I don't know, how much of the Philippines can you write about?* All of my fantasies are set elsewhere: Spain or Iceland or Greece. There are always small swaying boats and lights strung up above tables and old men with hairy knuckles pouring me purple wine leaning in to me because we have grown old in the same place and at the same time. There are fish and fisheries, oysters and oyster shells made to cup the ocean's liquor. I will spend days shirtless and happy with the wet sand drying on my feet. When my family looks at photos from the wedding in Italy they don't bother to think about why I wasn't there. It's *their* uncomfortable conversation, not mine. No one wants to talk about paperwork or changing legislation. It's been 30, 31, 32 years. That is that, I say. Until it no longer isn't. My brothers have been to Mexico, Italy, France, England, Cuba, Canada. "You'd love it there and there and there and there" I stare back and say nothing.

It was my first year at grad school when I began waking up in the mornings with a
weight pressing down on my chest. That was the year I began carrying small objects
around with me whenever I left the house as a way to fill up the sunken cavity: small
spoon, penny, pink paper clip bent but not broken. Further down, there is an
important system of deep ocean circulation. This circulation of deep ocean water
occurs because of differences in water density that arise from differences in salinity
and temperature. This water movement is referred to as thermohaline circulation.
Ocean water will become denser, and thus sink, if its salinity increases or its
temperature decreases. This happens in high-latitude ocean areas where the
water is cold and salinity increases when sea ice develops (the dissolved salts are
not taken up in the ice when water freezes, so the salinity of the remaining water
increases). The list of objects

on the ocean floor is inexhaustible: language, tea kettles, dominos, plastic kazoos, birth certificates, terra cotta pots, typewriters, rosaries, faceless coins, light bulbs, epigraphs, one mahogany bedpost, gold door knobs, dictionaries, zebra costume, Hanukkah candles, cassava, castanets, ligature, mannequins from Asia, cables, cords, bricks, scrap of chain-link fence, hooks, shark carcass, shop keys, teeth, unopened can of paint, the color orange, jar of honey, rusted chainsaw, chopsticks, cameras, hard drives, a no-name map, a mirror pointed skyward.

horizon — a permanent humiliation on the act of arrival
horizon — a permanent humiliation through the act of arrival
horizon — a permanent humiliation to the act of arrival

A boy inspects the foamy edge of a wave with his toes, lets go of his toy bucket, and rushes into the water. He swims out to touch the horizon. There, he looks over the edge. He points down, looks back, and says, *another world over there!* From where I am, the boy disappears.

Answer No

1a. Have you ever knowingly committed any crime of moral turpitude (including but not limited to theft, fraud, forgery) or a drug-related offense for which you have not been arrested?
Define forgery.
See "XXX-XX-0142"

[...]

4. Have you ever engaged in, conspired to engage in, or do you intend to engage in, or have you ever solicited membership or funds for, or have you through any means ever assisted or provided any type of material support to, any person or organization that has ever engaged or conspired to engage, in sabotage, kidnapping, political assassination, hijacking, or any form of terrorist activity?
Define kidnapping.
See "April 1984"

[...]

14. Do you plan to practice polygamy in the U.S.?
Define practice.
See "A Love Poem with a Hole in It"

[...]

15c. Do you intend to engage in the U.S. in any activity to violate any law prohibiting the export from the United States of goods, technology, or sensitive information?
Define sensitive information.
See "Balikbayan"

Acknowledgments

I haven't read Carlos Bulosan or José Rizal. I haven't read Jessica Hagedorn. I haven't read Patrick Rosal. I haven't read Rick Barot. I haven't read Nick Carbo. I googled Eileen Tabio, Gemino Abad, Michael Melo, Fatima Lim-Wilson, Virginia Cerenio but I haven't read any of them either. I'll probably like Catalina Cariaga. She wrote one book called *Cultural Evidence* and disappeared. I didn't know Randall Mann and Ronaldo Wilson were Filipino. Or half. I might have read them without knowing. I followed then unfollowed Oliver de la Paz on Instagram because I got bored or jealous seeing his kids at the pumpkin patch, opening presents, eating spaghetti. I think I might like Marc Gaba. He went to Iowa then quit Denver: *Part of the reason I left the Ph.D. program is that I felt like anything I could say would be treated as the thing said by "that guy from the islands." How insulting and misinformed, though easy to understand, because America tends to be locked in on itself as any center of the world, and the Philippines keeps representing itself as a tourist destination with beaches everywhere.* Interviewer: What are you going to do now? *I'm going to work on a painting. I think I hit upon a solution to introduce narrative to the process. As far as creation goes, that's the best thing that's happened today . . . to find where in that abstraction is the beginning and the end. Of course, it's going to be a process, because in abstraction, to finish is to make narrativity disappear.* I followed Barbara Jane Reyes for a while. I didn't *like* this post of hers but I've been thinking about it for days: *Here's the thing. You grow up as a Filipino in America, believing we are not represented in Literature. This is a problem and so you diss Literature. Then you learn that there are lots of Filipinos in America, representing in Literature. You make the decision, however, to continue dissing Literature. You make the decision not to read; you diss Filipinos in America in Literature. And then you go about your life pretending they don't exist, that they never existed in the first place. You are now part of the problem.* On every cover letter I've ever written for every school, every award, every scholarship, and every fellowship I make sure to say that I was born in the Philippines so the judges know that my white-sounding name belongs to me.

Frank Quizon Gray Jr. III

I practiced my father's signature
this morning. I practiced my

father's signature this morning.
He holds his pen softer than

me. He holds his pen softer
than me. His Q's, large and

open. His Q's, large and open.
His F's, like those telephone

poles. His F's, like those
telephone poles. His cursive

is beautiful. His cursive is so
so beautiful. The letters

are due tomorrow. The
letters are due tomorrow.

Birth Certificate

The pot boils. I reach deep

into the oven and scar the scarred part

of my arm. I place words

and words together,
          un-together, take apart,

to make an art from documents
that twin a life to mine.

It was 1984, 1978, 1997, I was 21, 18, I was born, I was six.

It's been 32, 37, 38, 39 years of verses and few refrains.

Immigration and Naturalization Services

ext. parking lot

The engine idle, we are six jackets huddled in the car staring at the building. We breathe and cloud the windows. You reach inside for the breakfast sandwiches and fried potatoes, wilting in their own trapped steam. Circles of oil stain the paper, inside then out. The word for lawyer in Tagalog and in Spanish is *abogado*. The news is full of other people's stories. It began to rain in IL, in WA, in TX, in FL, in CA, and in all the other states of America.

Immigration and Naturalization Services

exterior, parking lot

We are six jackets huddled in the car, the engine idle, the windows gray from our breathing. You reach inside a paper bag. The word for lawyer in Tagalog and in Spanish is *abogado*, the word for papers, *papeles*. We sit in silence, waiting for the news. The book does not want to end in rain. In IL, WA, TX, FL, and CA, it begins.

Immigration and Naturalization Services

exterior

The engine idle, we are six jackets in the car. Through the windows clouded by our breathing, we stare at the words on the building: IMMIGRATION AND NATURALIZATION SERVICES. Some citizens are natural; others are naturalized. The film is set in IL, WA, TX, FL, and CA. It can be shot anywhere.

Immigration and Naturalization Services

ext. parking lot

The car stalled, a circle of oil seeps into the concrete, the number six, a folder full of forms and letters, the breathing in, then out. You don't have papers. You don't know how to say it. You speak in the language you are learning to master. The doors of the building open. You watch as the others exit. Then, another word approaches.

Notes

p. 20: The ISBN numbers refer to Matthew Shenoda's *Somewhere Else* and from C. S. Giscombe's *Giscome Road*.

p. 21: "Balikbayan" is an erasure of a Wikipedia entry. The entry has been amended many times since.

p. 26: "A Migration" borrows a line from the Robert Haas poem "Art and Life."

p. 36: "d. 1997" borrows a phrase from a David Berman poem he read at St. Mary's College in 2001.

p. 65: "EXAQUA" takes its title from the "Notanda" section of M. NourbeSe Philip's *Zong!* The epigraph is from Jennifer S. Cheng's poem "How to Build an American Home" from *House A.*

pp. 66, 67, 68, 71, 72, and 74: The essay includes excerpts from an email conversation with Jennifer S. Cheng.

p. 68 (*There is a space . . .*): This passage is from Juliana Spahr's "Poem after September 11, 2001" from *This Connection of Everyone with Lungs.*

p. 74: This section borrows language from the textbook *McKnight's Physical Geography* by Darrel Hess.

p. 80: A portion of this is taken from an interview of Mark Gaba by Amy Wright from *Parcel Journal.*

Acknowledgments

Thank you to the following publications where these poems, in slightly different forms, have appeared:

Academy of American Poets: "Maid Poem #7: HR";

Ano Ba Zine: "Maid Poem #5: Rita";

Assaracus: "Maid Poem #1: The Housemaid," "Sapling," and "Love Poem with a Hole in It";

Colorado Review: "Maid Poem #2" and "Mackerel";

DIAGRAM: "EXAQUA";

Fourteen Hills: "PNW";

Nepantla: An Anthology Dedicated to Queer Poets of Color: "I-797-C";

Puerto del Sol: "In 'The Store with Beautiful Things'";

The Puritan: "April 1984" and "Across the Pacific Ocean";

The Rumpus: "I-797-C," "XXX-XX-0142," "On Translation," "Terminal Couplet," and "Crush, Supermarket, California";

Shade Journal: "Hindi Ko Alam Ng Sasabihin Ko";

Southern Humanities Review: "egress";

Small Po[r]tions: "Missing Document";

Transfer: "California Triptych" and "For Tanzania";

Tupelo Quarterly: "Balikbayan" and "Acknowledgments."

This book owes its gratitude to everyone who has taught me anything.

To all of the cooks, dishwashers, and friends who worked the long hours next to me in kitchens, thank you. Thank you for teaching me all of your languages. To everyone who has taken note of my writing or listened a little closer to an idea, thank you. To everyone who has read through these poems, invited me to read them out loud, and otherwise shared a space for writing and thinking to happen, thank you.

Matthew Shenoda, thank you for your countless hours of counsel and for showing me all the ways of being a poet. Camille Dungy, thank you for being present for me so early on, and especially for asking me about "the book" before I knew I was writing one.

To D.A. Powell, thank you for opening this door for me to walk through. I am so fortunate to have you by my side. Thank you for the generosity, intelligence, and care you've directed toward this book. To everyone at BOA Editions, Ltd., and especially Peter Conners, Ron Martin-Dent, Sandy Knight, and Richard Foerster who have made the process of producing this book a truly collaborative process, thank you. To Jonathan Molina-Garcia, dear friend, thank you for creating the beautiful image on the cover. To Christopher Soto, Eduardo C. Corral, and Barbara Jane Reyes, thank you all for giving your time and attention to my work.

Thank you to the amazing people at San Francisco State University and its Creative Writing Department: Truong Tran, Steve Dickison, Maxine Chernoff, and a special thank you to Heather June Gibbons.

To the many amazing teachers at City College of San Francisco, thank you. Thank you to Xochi Candelaria, Jennifer Worley, Ardel Thomas, Andrea Sanelli, and Rose Heller.

Thank you to T Clutch Fleischmann, Jennifer S. Cheng, and Chelsea Turowsky.

Thank you to the support from the Undocupoets fellowship, the Jack Kent Cooke Foundation, Columbia College Chicago, and Dara Wier and the Juniper Summer Writing Institute.

Thank you to Robert Uy and to everyone who continues to advocate for the rights of immigrants and their families in this county. A special thank you to everyone at Illinois Coalition of Immigrant and Refugee Rights in Chicago.

I dedicate this book to my family, especially to my parents whose lives, in part, I've made material. Thank you for everything.

To Crisby, my husband and my first reader: thank you. No one has been closer to me or this book and everything around it than you. You know. We have made a life together.

About the Author

Jan-Henry Gray was born in Quezon City, Philippines, and moved to California with his family when he was six years old. He grew up in Southern California and lived in San Francisco where he cooked in restaurants for more than twelve years. He received his BA in Creative Writing from San Francisco State University and his MFA in Poetry from Columbia College Chicago. Along with awards from the Jack Kent Cooke Foundation and the Academy of American Poets, he received the inaugural Undocupoets Fellowship. His work has been published in *Nepantla: An Anthology for Queer Poets of Color, The Rumpus, Tupelo Quarterly, Colorado Review, Fourteen Hills, Puerto del Sol, Southern Humanities Review*, and other journals. He lives in Chicago.

BOA Editions, Ltd.
The A. Poulin, Jr. New Poets of America Series

No. 1 *Cedarhome*
Poems by Barton Sutter
Foreword by W. D. Snodgrass

No. 2 *Beast Is a Wolf with Brown Fire*
Poems by Barry Wallenstein
Foreword by M. L. Rosenthal

No. 3 *Along the Dark Shore*
Poems by Edward Byrne
Foreword by John Ashbery

No. 4 *Anchor Dragging*
Poems by Anthony Piccione
Foreword by Archibald MacLeish

No. 5 *Eggs in the Lake*
Poems by Daniela Gioseffi
Foreword by John Logan

No. 6 *Moving the House*
Poems by Ingrid Wendt
Foreword by William Stafford

No. 7 *Whomp and Moonshiver*
Poems by Thomas Whitbread
Foreword by Richard Wilbur

No. 8 *Where We Live*
Poems by Peter Makuck
Foreword by Louis Simpson

No. 9 *Rose*
Poems by Li-Young Lee
Foreword by Gerald Stern

No. 10 *Genesis*
Poems by Emanuel di Pasquale
Foreword by X. J. Kennedy

No. 11 *Borders*
Poems by Mary Crow
Foreword by David Ignatow

No. 12 *Awake*
Poems by Dorianne Laux
Foreword by Philip Levine

No. 13 *Hurricane Walk*
Poems by Diann Blakely Shoaf
Foreword by William Matthews

Colophon

BOA Editions, Ltd., a not-for-profit publisher of poetry and other literary works, fosters readership and appreciation of contemporary literature. By identifying, cultivating, and publishing both new and established poets and selecting authors of unique literary talent, BOA brings high-quality literature to the public. Support for this effort comes from the sale of its publications, grant funding, and private donations.

—

*The publication of this book is made possible, in part,
by the support of the following patrons:*

Anonymous
Angela Bonazinga & Catherine Lewis
Susan DeWitt Davie
Geffrey Davis
James Long Hale
Keetje & Sarah Kuipers, *in memory of Julie Shaffer*
Joe McElveney
Dan Meyers, *in honor of J. Shepard Skiff*
Boo Poulin
Deborah Ronnen
Steven O. Russell & Phyllis Rifkin-Russell
William Waddell & Linda Rubel